Splatoon 2
Coloring Book

Smiling Kid

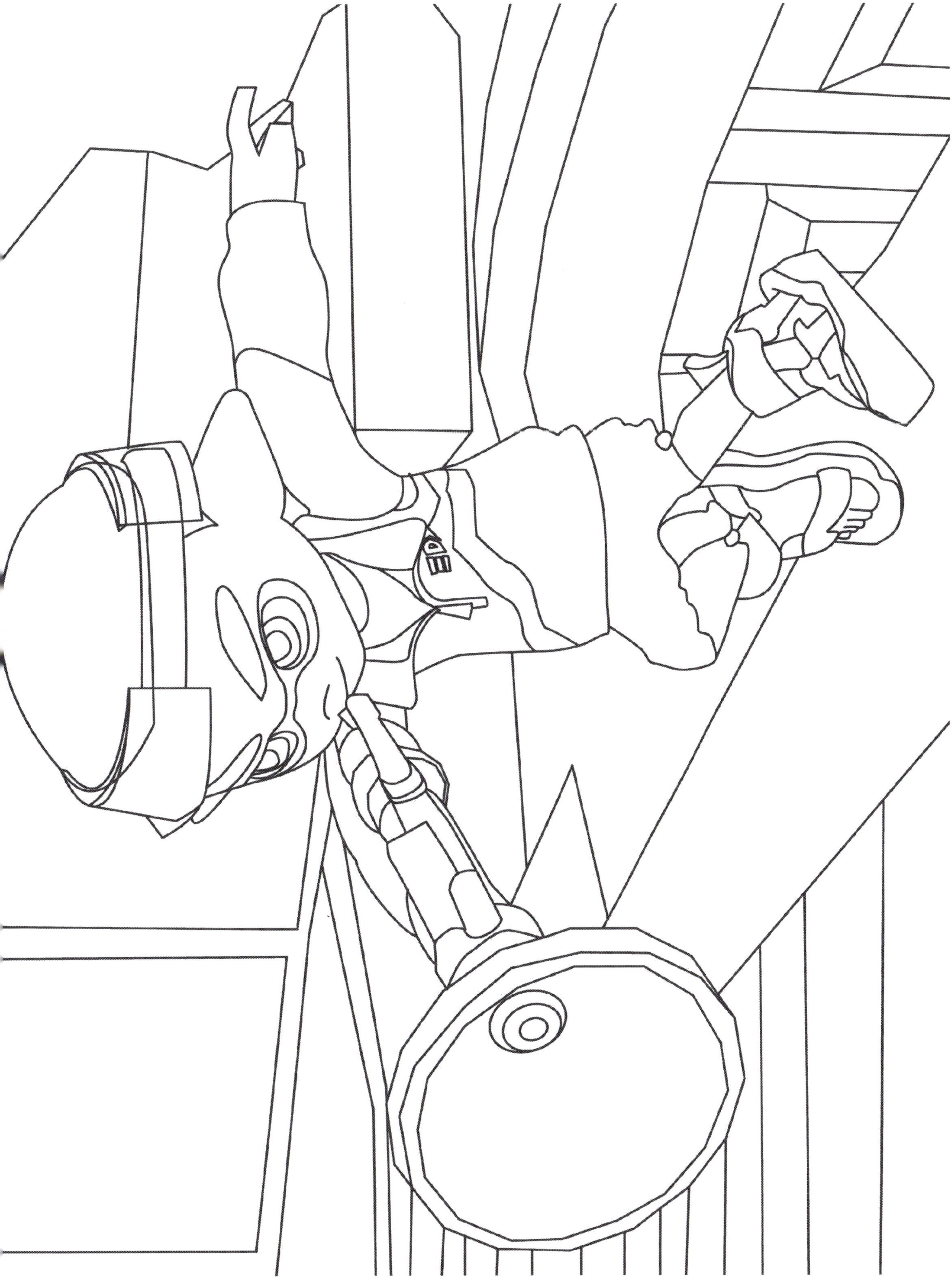

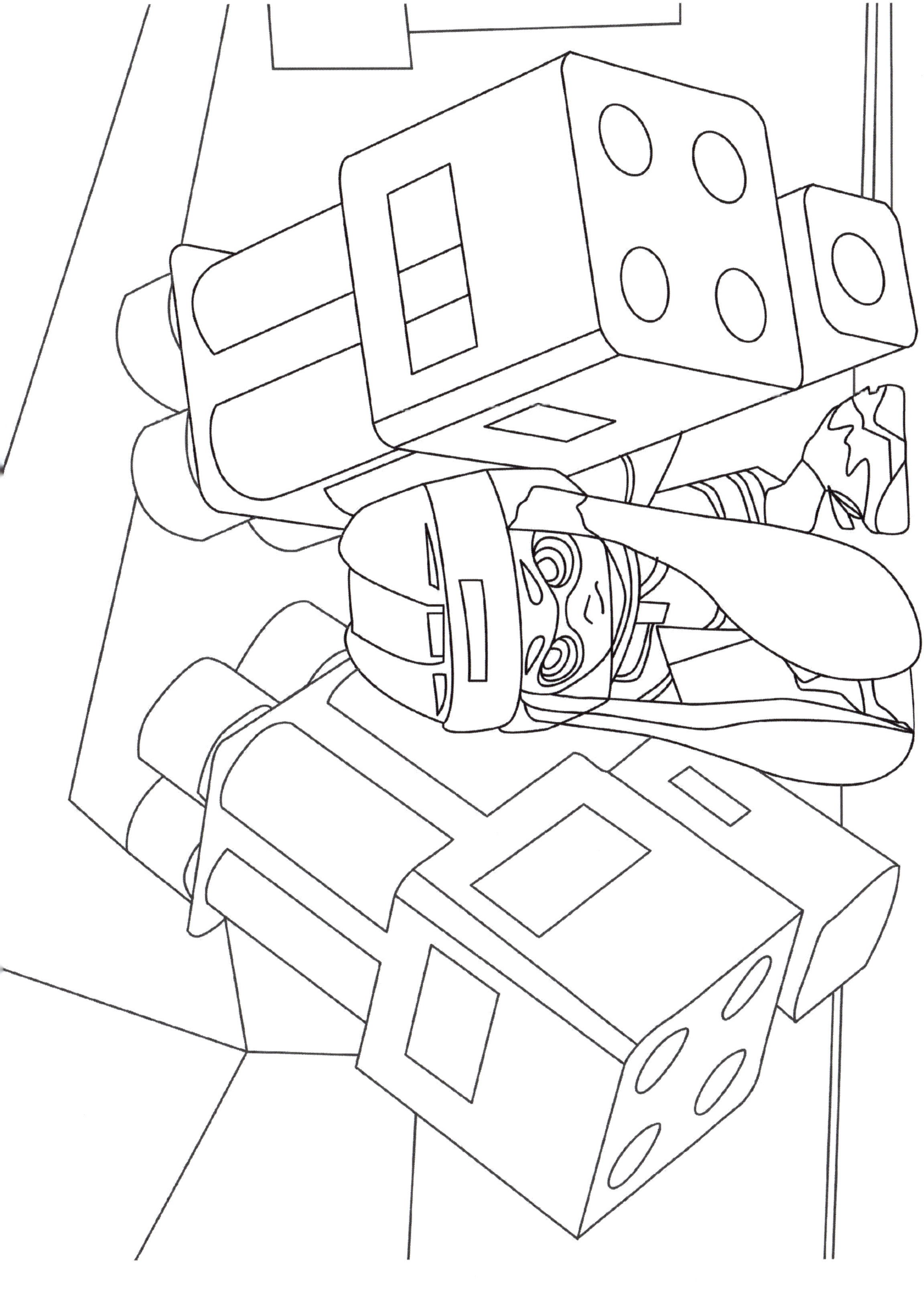

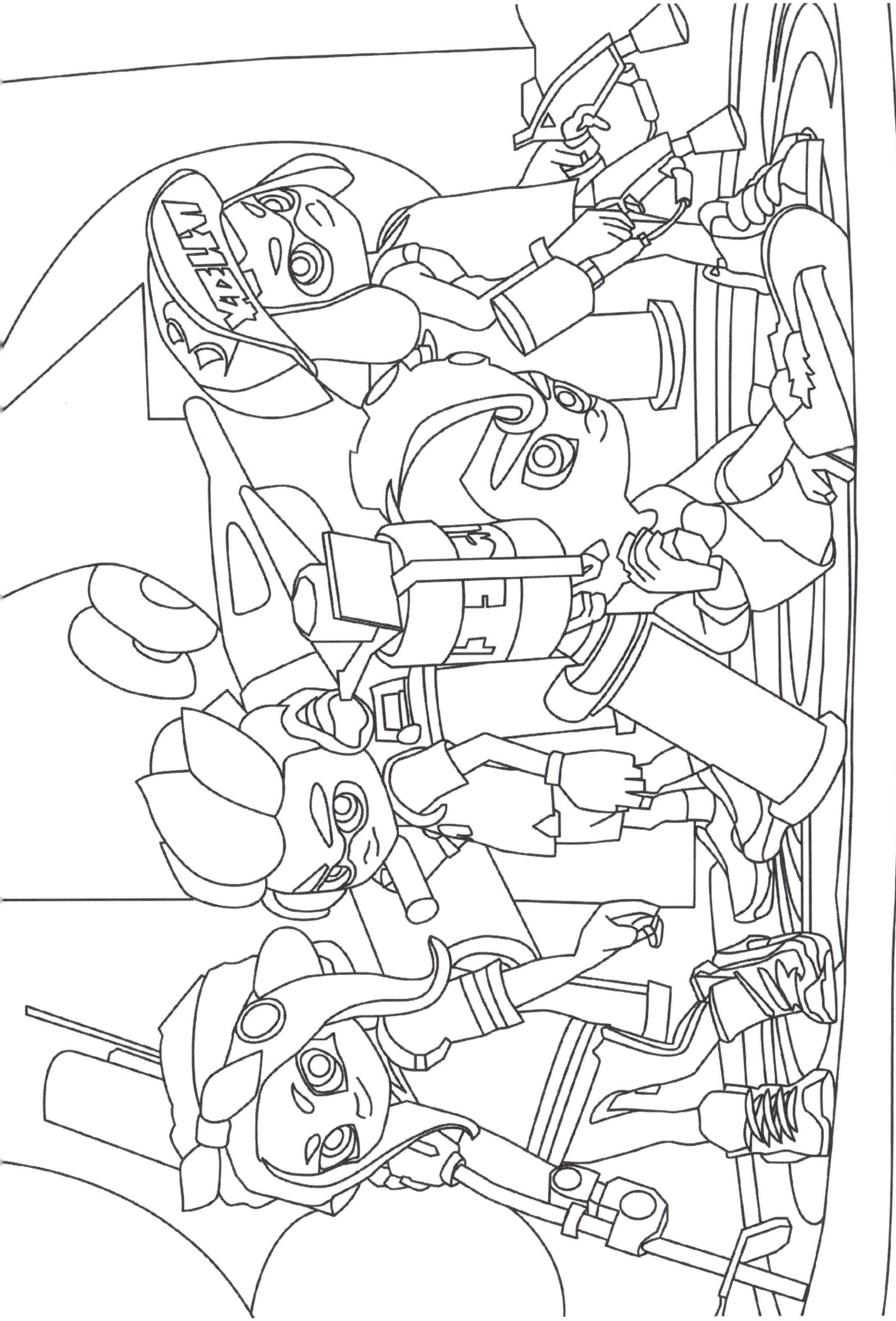

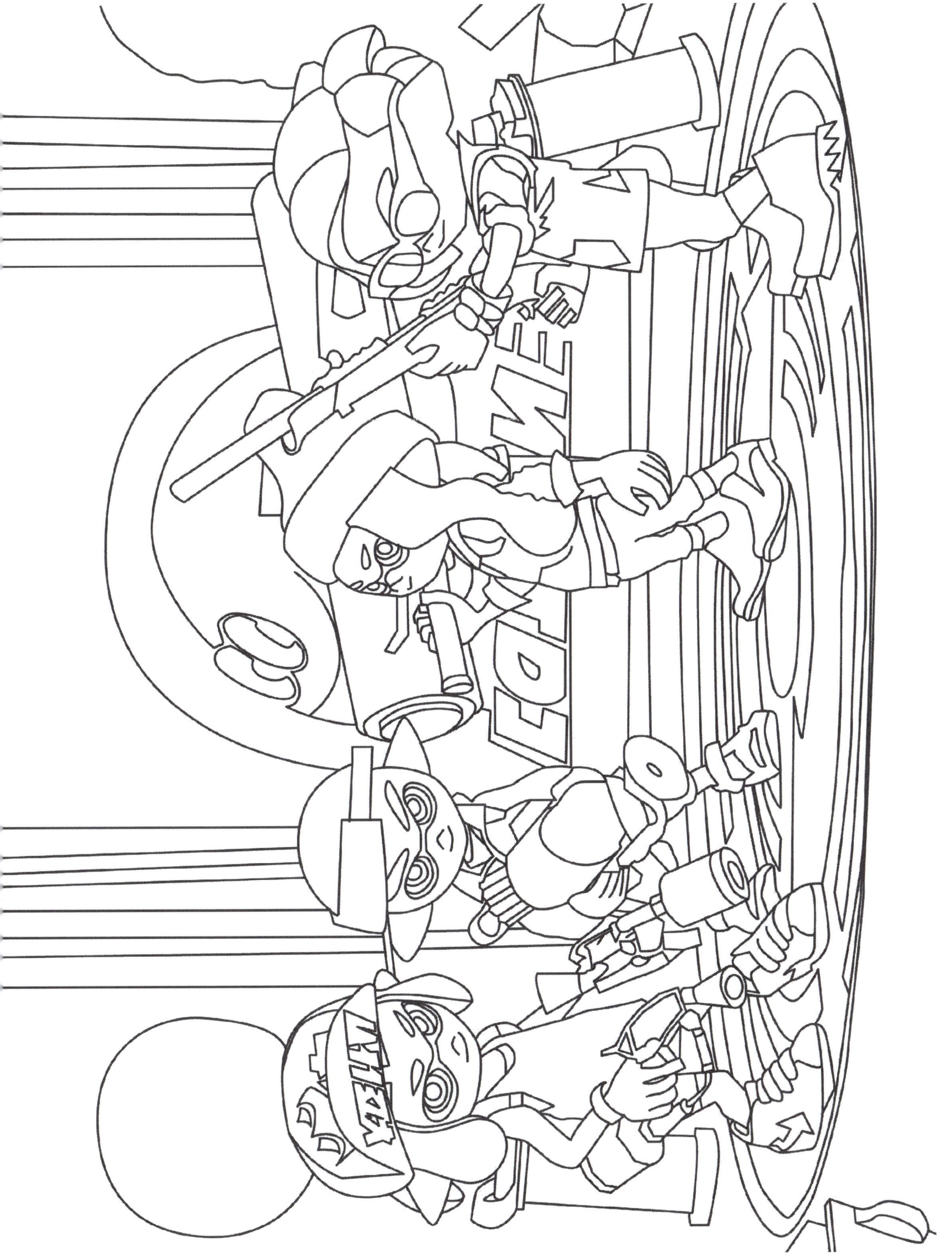

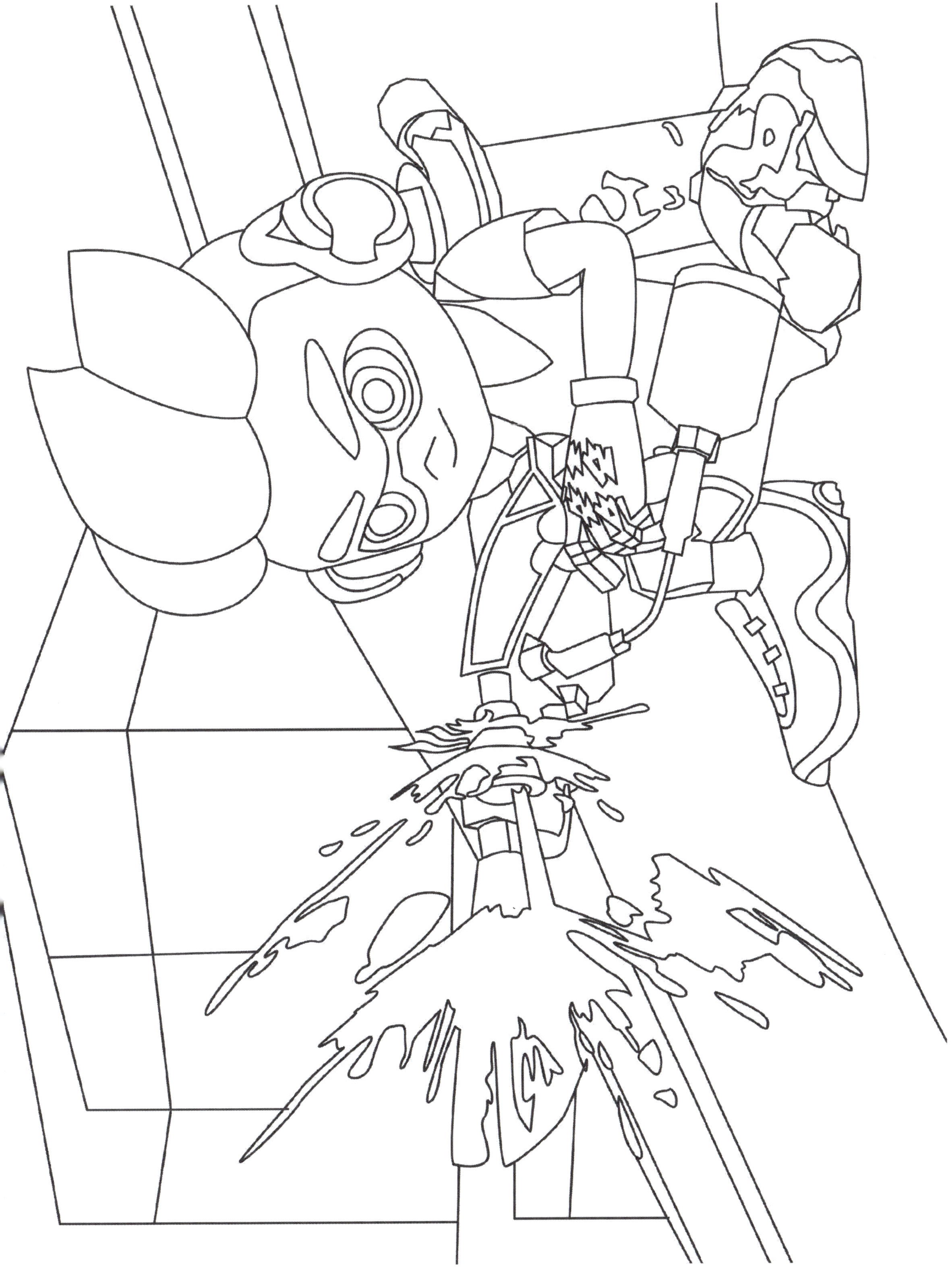

Made in the USA
Middletown, DE
31 August 2020

17370674R00031